TO Chris & Lindsay
with love. mom ♡

Dianne's Doghouse
Doggie Devotions

Published by Living History Productions
302 Center Street
Ashland, Ohio 44805

Printed by BookMasters, Inc.
30 Amberwood Parkway
Ashland, Ohio 44805

Cover Design and All Artwork by Dianne Hammontree
Ashland, Ohio

Edited by Julie Donatini
Ashland, Ohio

Library of Congress Control Number: 2010922949
ISBN 978-0-9761327-1-4

With love, I dedicate this
book to my grandchildren
and the love of my life,
Jesus Christ.

Table of Contents

Table of Contents

Our writing comes from our being. In her book of gentle wisdom, Dianne brings a sensitivity and understanding for "wounded spirits" and how the response of cherished companion dogs can transform and heal. Dogs often attend to our unspoken wounds. They sense a need and enter a person's space slowly, respectfully. They nurture by intimacies openly given.

The instincts of these dogs are remarkable metaphors of love. They are defined by loyalty, acceptance, forgiveness, and a desire to please and serve. These companions are so formed by the Hand of the Father that they do, and are, what He made them to be…followers of his plan.

The bonds of affection animal friends can form are able to open hearts closed for many years. I recall in the movie "As Good as It Gets," the character played by Jack Nicholson finds a place for a dog where he initially could allow no human.

The phrase, "I wish I could be the person my dog thinks I am," captures a profound nuance of canine love. While at the same time, it mirrors the power of how, when someone thinks well of us, we rise to that belief.

Dianne's sweet tempered book invites us into her world. Her stories carry with each unfolding a unique blend of disclosure and promise. She reminds us of God's wisdom through the words of the Psalms and New Testament. Dianne talks to us through stories and drawings about the ability of God's creatures to bring joy, comfort, peace and friendship even to the most broken of hearts.

You will be touched as you read these stories and they may even offer a gentle healing to your own soul.

By Martha Phillips Jorden
Hospice of North Central Ohio
Grief Counselor

Who is a happy person?
…a child building a sand castle
…a doctor saving a life
…a mother bathing her baby
…a carpenter whistling after a job well done
…a master petting his dog
(Notice that not one answer involves fame, money or power)
…a child praying
…a friend listening
…a master and his dog walking in the woods
…a man who is the covering for his family
…a husband who warms his wife's heart

Happiness is a byproduct. When you seek it directly, you never find it. Happiness rubs off when you do something for others. We can control our own state of happiness. It is not the result of circumstances. It is how you look at what happens to you that makes you happy or unhappy.

The Bible teaches us about happiness:
…love God first
…serve others joyfully
…practice humility, patience, prayer and worship
…study God's word

I remember, years ago, when I was about 11; one of my happy times was when I was outside my house with my dog, Jet. Jet was coal-black with white paws and a white diamond on her forehead. She was pudgy but could run like the wind.

We were in the back yard and I was hanging upside down from our old transparent apple tree with my skinned and bruised knees hooked over a low, thick branch. I was swinging back and forth, my ponytails dangling like frayed ropes. As I hummed "Jesus loves me," Jet kept her eyes glued to mine.

My dog was there; God was there; my spirit was content. I had no money, no fame, no power; but I was happy.

I believe that happiness is at our fingertips and may be only a dedicated prayer away.

Though I grew up with a little dog, I had never been an adult pet owner. My first puppy, Rusty, was a Cairn Terrier. He was a bouncy terrier and a strong-willed boy. I made major parenting mistakes as training progressed. Whenever Rusty did something wrong, I spoke very loudly, "Bad dog, Rusty." Because he was young and untrained, he heard "bad dog" a lot.

Like all puppies, Rusty loved to chew. His favorite chew toys were my shoes, and soon I had not one whole pair of matching shoes. I scolded him and showed him what was left of the shoes and again told him he was a "bad dog." He looked at me with his big, brown puppy eyes and huddled in the corner of the kitchen.

Poor Rusty heard those horrible words more than he heard the comforting words of "good dog." I was frustrated and didn't hug him as often. His little spirit was breaking. Finally, I asked for advice:
1. Don't yell
2. Praise often
3. Say "Good dog!" often
4. Hug often

I took this advice and soon Rusty was joyful again. He could hear and see that I loved him. His chewing stopped. He knew he was a "good boy" and was loved unconditionally.

Luckily, Rusty came along before my children. Rusty taught me to be kind to my children, co-workers and friends. He taught me that we can be overwhelmed by our mistakes. He taught me ***not*** to crush another's spirit.

I believe we would all be crushed if we knew the full extent of our sins all at once. God understands this and refines and corrects us gently.

I love to hear that still small voice, "Good girl, Dianne." God is a God of encouragement. We all need to lift each other up and our animals, too.

When my girls were four and five years old, I decided they needed a puppy. It was time for them to learn to care for one of God's fuzzy little creatures; to be kind, to feed and water and to learn a sense of responsibility at this young age.

A Sheltie seemed to be the right choice—small enough so the girls didn't get knocked over, but large enough to play with.

On Christmas Eve, after the girls were in bed, the baby Sheltie arrived. She was very shy and cuddly. I caged her and kept her in a room far away from the girls' bedroom. On Christmas morning, I fed and walked the puppy, put a red bow around her neck and placed her under the tree. When the girls came into the living room and saw the puppy, they giggled with delight.

All day they cared for their new friend, bathing her, gently feeding her tidbits of dog food and snuggling all together at naptime. They named her "Christmas Joy." About 7 p.m. Christmas night, the girls burst into tears and were so inconsolable with blubbering sobs that I couldn't figure out where their pain was coming from. Finally, they calmed down and asked when Santa was going to take Joy back to the North Pole. They thought Santa was only going to let them have their gift for one day.

How do I explain this?

I said, "Daughters, you have been given your puppy as a gift to keep just as God gives grown-up people gifts. Remember the Bible story we read the other night about the talents? The Master had three servants. He gave each servant a gift of money. Two of the servants doubled their money. The third servant buried his money and lost it. You have been given this puppy as a gift. If you are mean and mistreat her, you could lose her. But, if you take good care of her, God will allow you to move on to greater things your heart's desire."

The puppy helped my girls grow up. She helped ease them into the role of becoming moms.

Bathing a reluctant puppy was good training for bathing a squirming, uncooperative baby.

Disciplining Joy with a rolled up newspaper gave them confidence to discipline a wayward toddler. God, in His wisdom, gave my girls Christmas Joy before he gave them children of their own. God used a lesser thing to prepare them for more.

Who knows what amazing things God may have in store for my daughters who are faithful to Him.

You have been faithful with a few things; I will put you in charge of many things. Matthew 25:21.

My dog, Jesse, and I were excited to begin our direct-patient care service as brand new Hospice volunteers. To prepare for our first patient, I gave Jesse a bath with cherry vanilla shampoo, gave her a good brushing and placed her identification necklace and red bandana around her neck. We proudly walked to the nursing home and located the correct room. When I saw the gentleman's name on the door, my heart stopped beating.

Don, the meanest man in the world, was Jesse's first Hospice patient.

About two months earlier, Don came to look at one of my remodeled houses with his daughter. His daughter loved the house and wanted to sign the paperwork to purchase it. Don began verbally ripping the house apart—inch by inch—electrical, plumbing, paint, carpentry, etc., etc., etc. He not only insulted my hard work, but attacked my character as well. I was too dumbfounded by this evil string of abusive words to reply or to stand up for myself. By the time Don and his daughter left, I was crushed to the floor.

Jesse and I met our weekly Hospice obligation with Don for months.

Usually, Hospice is only responsible for a patient deemed terminal for a six-month period, then staff and volunteers are called off. After six months, Don was still alive and stable. We continued our visits anyway.

One afternoon I received an emergency phone call from the nursing home. "Please bring Jesse—quick!" the nurse said. "Your patient is hysterical and violent. We have tried everything to calm him down and nothing is working. BRING JESSE NOW!"

Jesse and I entered the room to find Don totally out of control. His sweet little wife, Daisy, couldn't calm him either. Even though he was older and weak, he could send anyone flying across the room with his thrashing arms and legs.

Jesse slowly walked over to Don's bed and waited. His wild eyes spotted her and he waited. She laid her head on the bed. He stroked her ears. Ever so slowly he came back to reality without hurting Jesse. As he petted her, he talked and talked and talked. As it turned out, he had just realized that he was going to die and did not know where he was going—heaven or hell. Don had spent years ignoring God, feeling lonely to the core, feeling unsafe and unprotected. Life was such a frightening place because he thought we all were just thrown out there with no purpose, no plan, no direction and no help.

Little by little, with great trepidation and embarrassment, he began to entertain the possibility of God's existence. He was amazed to find out that even after all this time of pushing God away, God had never gone anywhere. All he had to do was open his ears and his heart and find God, right there waiting.

Don did die shortly after this amazing journey, and Jesse and I felt privileged to have had the pleasure of knowing the "meanest man" as our patient.

Jesse was tested by Therapy Dog International in Wooster, Ohio when she was two years old. She passed the most rigorous testing—except "Sit." The officer felt so bad that she couldn't pass Jesse for not sitting that she took time out of her busy schedule to chat, hoping Jesse would get bored and sit down. Jesse sat, finally, and passed the test!

One rainy, cold day I took Jesse to a nursing home to visit a friend's mom. The mom and I began talking and when I looked around to check on Jesse, I found that she was gone from the room.

I excused myself and went looking for the absent dog. Jesse was way down the hall in a room with two cute little older ladies— one smiling and one in tears.

Did my gentle Jesse bite the crying lady? Heavens no! Here is the rest of the story.

Jesse knows when a human is in need. She sensed this in the nursing home and sought out her person. It was Mabel's first day in the home and she was very scared. On this dreary, cold day, Jesse peeked into the room, gently took hold of her sleeve and walked her down the hall to Evelyn's room so Evelyn could be Mabel's new friend.

Evelyn was smiling at Jesse's act of kindness and Mabel was crying because a dog could be so kind and compassionate. Jesse's mission was accomplished, so she took my sleeve and led me out the door to go home for dinner.

Jesse is older now and slowing down a bit. She still visits young and old and continually amazes me how she looks into their souls and knows their hearts. Often times she reminds me of our God and how He knows and loves us just as we are and how He always sends random acts of kindness our way.

As a substitute teacher, many surprises happen even if it is the first day on the job. One day I was subbing at a school for at-risk teens.

One particular student, Nikki, scrawny and fearful, came to the door of my classroom. I believed that if she felt cornered, she could be aggressive. Could she have been on the streets as a fifteen year old, starved for food and love, forced to take care of herself?

Since Jesse, my red Golden Retriever, was a therapy dog, I was allowed to take her with me to teach. Jesse and I welcomed Nikki and showered her with kindness.

The first thing Nikki did was swing her right leg backwards so she could kick Jesse in the chest. I blocked the kick and told her if she ever tried to hurt my dog again she would live to regret it! She growled profanities at us, stormed into the classroom and plopped down on an old couch with a grunt. Her arms were crossed over her chest in defiance and her glare revealed a hardened heart.

"God, please give me the strength to get through this day," I prayed. My prayer had no sooner left my lips when I looked out of the corner of my eye and saw Jesse casually walking over to Nikki. Gently, Jesse sat down and lovingly looked at Nikki. Nikki scooted over to the left a little. Jesse did too. Nikki moved further to the left. Then Jesse, who had never been on a piece of furniture climbed upon the couch. Nikki moved left again so that she practically melted into the armrest of the couch. Jesse put her head in Nikki's lap.

For what seemed like hours, dog and child were embodied in a time capsule. Neither of them moved. Then I saw a flicker of light in Nikki's eyes. Silently, one hand unwound itself and she laid a finger on Jesse's head. Trying to look as if she didn't care and failing miserably, Nikki relaxed and let the palm of her hand rest on Jesse's back.

They connected: mind and heart.

God works in mysterious ways. We don't need to understand them anymore than Nikki did. Probably for the first time in her life she experienced unconditional love through Jesse. I hope someday she will experience my Master's love and discover that He will give her what she really needs and that He will do what is best for her. Beyond all mystery is the mercy of God.

I still pray for Nikki even though it has been ten years since our classroom experience. She was literally a homeless fifteen year old. She had been evicted from her mother's house, aunt's house, Grandma's house and foster home. I hope she is okay and that she will remember Jesse.

"For it is God who works in you..."
Philippians 2:13

Jesse, my red Golden Retriever, and Meggie, my daughter's golden, Golden Retriever, were best friends. When Jen (my daughter) and I remodeled houses together, the two dogs would always accompany us in the truck, first to the coffee shop, then on to work.

We learned a lot from Jesse and Meggie over the years. They showed us what it meant to be faithful friends. They stood by us at work, when we were tired and frustrated and in sickness and in health.

They not only provided a special quiet comfort to us, but also to my dad as he dealt with prostate cancer.

Dad was seventy-three years old when he was first diagnosed with cancer. He refused surgery but agreed to radiation treatments. After thirty-nine back-to-back trips to the hospital, Dad went into remission. Four years later the cancer came back with a vengeance.

Dad would lie on the living room couch wrapped in a blanket. Jesse and Meggie would curl up beside him during our lunch break, then again after dinner.

Mom's church family, Hospice, and

Jen and I helped cook and clean, but Mom took the brunt of caring for Dad. She had to help dress him, feed him, get him to the bathroom and medicate him. She had to do every little personal thing for him that he'd always done for himself. Mom did all of this faithfully, without complaining and with a grateful heart.

When Jesse and Meggie stayed close to Dad, Mom felt free to do laundry, fix dinner or to take a long hot shower and put on her pajamas. She knew that if Dad needed her, one of the dogs would run and fetch her immediately.

As grateful as Mom was for the help from Jesse, Meggie, Jen and I or for the encouragement from her friends or church family, Mom knew that there were times when only one Friend could help. God was always there to lift her up and comfort her. During Dad's last couple of months on earth, with Jesse and Meggie by his side, we talked about God, heaven and angels. Dad saw angels. He described them in great detail. Sometimes he would talk to the dogs, sometimes to me and sometimes to the comforting spirit invisible to me.

Because of Dad, I learned how important it is to stay connected to the lives of others. Procrastination and busy schedules can keep us from following through with the tugs of our heart. It is easy to think that tomorrow we will have time to visit that friend or check on our older neighbor. Time passes and the visit or call is never done.

Be a loyal and faithful friend.

Visit your friends and sit by their side like Jesse and Meggie did for my Dad.

Jesse was about ten years old (and Jeff three) when I worked at a community art center with at-risk teens. Twice a week the dogs would accompany me to the center and do their therapy dog job of visiting, hugging, eating and pretending to be large, furry pillows for the kids to rest their heads on while doing homework.

This homey atmosphere of dogs, homework and warm cookies worked wonders on the teens, so much so that I thought maybe their guardians might like to visit the center to discuss what their teens were learning. (I use the word "guardian" because most of the kids did not live with a traditional family member).

Anyway, back to the dogs, specifically, Jesse. Jesse longed to be close to me. I was her special person, the gal around whom her whole life revolved. The best place for her to be—where she felt the most comfortable, content and loved—was close to me, her loving master and friend.

One day in the fall, I scheduled several conferences with the teens and their guardians. The appointments went well.

Jeff and Jesse were at the art center hanging with the kids in the basement while I had conferences in the sanctuary upstairs.

Apparently Jesse realized I was absent from her and went out the open door to find me and disappeared. We all left the building to search for her, calling her name and asking neighbors to help.

I felt as helpless as I had ever felt. I paced up and down the streets of town. I drove my truck all night through the town and into the country.

Two days later Jesse was still missing. I had already called the dog pound but decided to call again.

"Do you have a beautiful, old, reddish Golden Retriever there?" I asked.

"The dog catcher brought her in two days ago," they said.

I could not believe this! I rushed to the pound and there was Jesse, covered in saliva, scared, sad and lonely, her collar hanging on the cage door. Her collar had my address, phone number and her therapy dog tag on it! And they didn't even call!

They took Jesse out of the cage, and

she whimpered and wiggled her body and tried to crawl onto my lap like she was an eight week old puppy.

I knelt in front of her and we looked at each other for a long time. Then she dropped her head and pushed its crown directly against my chest. "You are the best," I whispered in her ear. She raised her head and laid her cheek against mine.

This separation from my dog reminded me of my longing to be close to God, my loving Master and Friend. I know the best place in the world to be—where I should feel the most comfortable, content and loved. Pursuing closeness with Him is challenging because God is invisible and only perceived by faith. He is not someone I could snuggle up to and rest my head on His lap like Jesse could with me. Sometimes, just like when Jesse and I were physically apart, there are times when I feel spiritually apart from God. Just like Jesse wanting to be physically close to me, I must take certain actions to restore my spiritual closeness with God.

We have His assurance. If we believe that Jesus is in our heart, God promises that nothing can ever separate us from His love.

Red and yellow, black and white.
They are precious in His sight.

Sometimes Jeff, my white Golden Retriever, didn't know what to give, so he gave himself. One day this one small giving act had a huge impact on a thirteen-year-old girl named Kristin. Jeff's act of appreciation affirmed his connection to her. He validated her. He expanded who she was. He helped deepen her spirit. This one ordinary moment turned into an extraordinary day, a praiseful day.

Kristin came to my after-school program with a downcast, sad demeanor. She appeared to have severe emotional scars from her past. I figured if I were patient and gave her lots of love and care, she would get better in time. Yet, despite my love, those scars remained.

Jeff accompanied me on an ordinary day to the after-school session. Jeff, a certified therapy dog, tugged at his leash as if to say, "Let's get going, mom, I have work to do." Jeff had been a smart, energetic pup who breezed through obedience training. His big brown eyes could melt the hardest of hearts. He became certified on his first birthday.

After Jeff and I entered the building,

he trotted over to a far corner where Kristin was sitting on the floor and would not budge. Kristin had her head down on her bent knees. Jeff snuggled up to her and put his chin on her shoulder. Kristin quietly put her tiny arm around him.

As I left the two alone and went on to teach the other fifteen teens, I caught a glimpse of Kristin stroking Jeff's coat. As I watched, she began quietly talking to him using no periods or commas. The words just flowed out of her like rushing water on a waterfall. I quickly called for a counselor to witness this breakthrough and when the counselor arrived, she and I tiptoed closer to Kristin and Jeff, hoping to get a glimpse of Kristin's tortured and troubled mind.

Unbelievable incidents from her past were revealed as Jeff leaned in closer and loved her more. I found the innocence of Kristin's soul to be a revelation. Because Jeff shared his perfect innocence and loyalty and gave Kristin a gift of affection, she was able to open the flood gates, verbalize her feelings and hurts and disappointments and finally receive the much needed professional help she deserved. The counselor said Kristin had been severely depressed for months and that they had tried everything, without any hope for a breakthrough. Jeff broke through, though.

Who would have known that Jeff could have made such a big difference in a child's life? But, I guess this is true for all of us—dog or human.

If we ask God to give us opportunities to help people, He will lead us where we are needed.

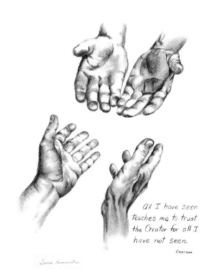

All I have seen
teaches me to trust
the Creator for all I
have not seen.

Emerson

In 2003, I began a journey into the "valley of the shadow of death"—my 35 year marriage was ending.

Since I had no money and nowhere to go, the basement became my temporary home. God held me close during those stressful months, and He sent me an angel: a dog-angel.

Dusty, the dog, followed me home on one of my lowest days. She stayed in the basement beside me and laid her head in my lap as I cried and cried. Within two weeks, I found her a new home, moved her in and hugged her goodbye.

Caring Christians enfolded me with their prayers, encouragement and counsel, yet I missed my angel. Jeff and Jesse were, of course, always close, but there was something very spiritual about Dusty.

One month later, standing outside my basement window was Dusty. She pranced into the basement and looked into my eyes for what seemed like hours.

I told her that I would be okay, that in time, I would be healed. Dusty took in every word and never took those beautiful and trusting eyes off me.

She left me that night and as she headed out the door and into the woods, she looked back, winked and disappeared from my life forever.

I think of Dusty often—about how she appeared when life seemed so hopeless, and I marvel at God's timing and at the precious gift He gave to me.

"If I rise on the wings of dawn, if I settle on the far side of the sea, even there Your hand will guide me; Your right hand will hold me fast!"
Psalm 139:9-10

I have been privileged to go on two mission trips to the Appalachian country of Kentucky. And amidst the poverty and unemployment, God was there; with the people, with their environment, with their animals. On my first trip to Kentucky, God sent a little homeless dog my way.

On the first morning, I went for a 5:30 a.m. walk. Through the mist, came an animal that looked like a coyote or a wolf. It headed straight for me at a full run. Great! I'll be fresh meat for this critter! No one from our church group even knows I am out here!

Thankfully, the "wolf" was a little dog that rolled over on her back to get her tummy scratched. Every morning she came to walk with me—except Thursday. I asked an older man if he knew of her. He did, but said the dog had gotten hit by a pick-up truck Wednesday night. He said she was really hurt.

After work, I went looking for her and found her in some bushes, still alive, but in bad shape. Friday morning, I gently lifted her up, put her in my truck and brought her home.

I got rid of the ticks, fleas, worms, matted fur and dirt. She was bathed, fed, walked, loved on and named Joy. I found a great home for her.

One day, before Joy went to her new home, we were walking down our street when she suddenly jumped upon an embankment, rolled upside down in the morning dew and quietly observed the sun and the birds, the trees and the sky. And she smiled.

Most of us forget to notice these free joys in life. This puppy reminded me of God's unconditional love and how to live in the present moment.

Maybe all of us should try rolling over in the sweet-smelling grass or on the white glistening snow. Maybe if we learned the lessons of the puppy, we would treat others kindly, we would help those in need, we would enjoy our families, friends and community even more.

Many of us have tried things we could have failed at—starting a new business, comforting an ill friend, chairing a committee or rescuing a puppy—but we went ahead and tried to do things so we could learn to improve ourselves and to grow as individuals.

We need to push ourselves to try new things. When the sting of failure hits—try again.

I love the saying of the Appalachia people: "If hard times never kissed you, you ain't lived."

Both hard times and good times will come our way.

Get stronger in the hard times and enjoy the good times.

I love the people God has placed in my life, and I thank Him for the puppies He has sent my way and for the lessons they have taught me.

Jeff, our big white Golden Retriever, is a very empathetic boy. If he thinks I am upset, he tries to comfort me. He will paw at me, lick my hand or lay his head on my lap and gaze up at me with those dark, soulful eyes. Sometimes I even get a big wet kiss. This is Jeff's way of giving me a hug and showing me how much he cares. I have seen him do this with others also.

One day, Jeff, Jesse and I walked up to the nursing home so Jesse could visit her Hospice patient, Gladys. As we entered the home, "The Cat" greeted us, took one long look at the giant dogs and then ran for safety. "The Cat" knew that Jesse considered cats sort of like over-sized dog biscuits—snack food. Eventually, we made our way down the long hallway and received a warm welcome from Gladys.

Gladys was very talkative, so I had to stay focused on the conversation. Many times, as patients would pet Jesse, they would share deep emotional joys, fears or concerns. This was one of those days for Gladys. About fifteen minutes into our conversation, I sensed that Jeff was not in the room any longer. I tied Jesse to Gladys' bedpost and began searching for Jeff.

From down the hallway, came a very distinct "ooh" from a large group of people. Oh, no! Jeff! I humbly entered the room and saw Jeff sitting beside an older, bedfast gentleman. About twenty people were around the gentleman's bed, crying and laughing at the same time. "I'm so sorry," I said as I attempted to retrieve Jeff. "No, no," they all chimed in at once, "You see, Dad knew he was dying and would see Jesus very soon. Then here comes this big beautiful angel-dog who gently entered this room, walked quietly up to Dad, looked lovingly at him and then planted a big, wet, sloppy kiss right on his lips. We all decided this was the best present Dad could have received before heavens gates opened to take him in. Thank you!"

Our dogs seem to know that when someone is hurting the most important thing they can do is to be there. They do not know what is wrong but that does not stop them from reaching out. They just offer themselves.

The Bible tells us that the apostle John was like that. John kept watch with his Lord at the foot of the cross. He could not take Christ's pain away—but he was there. Neither our dogs nor our friends and loved ones can be with us constantly, but God can.

Be there and care in His name.

Still Life

Towards the end of Jesse's life, she was blind, deaf and feeble in body and mind. She would wander in the backyard disoriented and lost, yet not far from her favorite resting place in the office at the Bed & Breakfast. I would find her in a secluded spot, usually in the hot sun, panting, hungry and thirsty. When this happened, I would help her stand up and gently lead her inside the house where food and water awaited her.

Reflecting on Jesse made me consider how my God had often found me wandering lost and disoriented, panting and weary, hungry for spiritual food and living water. During these times when things did not make sense in my life, God would say, "Hello, it's God talking, just listen." God has always had a hand on my life, but when my husband and I started the Bed & Breakfast, it felt as though God was more active and obviously more present. He prodded and whirled my thoughts and made me listen to Him. He murmured to me all the time.

Sometimes, when I wanted to roll myself up into a ball and curl up in the backyard like Jesse did until things got circumstantially better, I would shout, "Okay God, I'm calling on you: Talk to me." I could count on Him to stay with me just like Jesse knew that I would never leave her. I would always lift her out of the hot sun when she was too weak to move herself and place her in the shade with food and water.

I always assumed my faith was part of me, like the color of my eyes. Virtually fixed. But in my 50's, divorced and orphaned and starting a new life, I discovered that my faith wasn't like the color of my eyes. It was more like a seed planted in a garden or a newly planted tree. Without proper attention the seed withers without anyone even noticing—not even me.

Faith—my faith needs only this message: JESUS LOVES ME.

A message simple and profound. A message I need to hear over and over.

God will lift me up and feed me, just like I lifted up Jesse.

Jeff was our Golden Retriever. He was such a handsome boy; massive shoulders, large square head, beautiful white fur. He was truly magnificent, yet Jeff's identity did not come mainly from his looks. It came from his unique personality and from being our boy. Everyone in our community knew who Jeff was and that he was owned by the Hammontrees. Occasionally, he got lost.

One day he got lost in the wee hours of the morning—just slipped out the back door before we got our walking shoes on. We looked everywhere for two hours then came home to check the answering machine.

The local hardware store had called. We rushed over and found the owner, Mike, with Jeff. Mike had heard a dog barking continuously in the "refrigerator and stove" graveyard behind the store. He opened the door and yelled, "Sit!" Jeff sat. Then he yelled, "Quit barking!" Jeff quit barking. (Mike jokingly asked if we would teach his kids a few commands). He knew this well-behaved dog had to be ours. Anytime Jeff got lost, someone always brought him back. He belonged to us. We belonged to him.

Jeff has passed away, but I have wondered what would happen if he got lost today. What if his tags were old and faded and the rescuer could not read them? If they had to depend on his tags to identify him, they might not know he was Jeff.

We have dog tags too: fingerprints. Fingerprints help identify us. I had to be fingerprinted when Jeff became a therapy dog. I went to the hospital and a very nice lady rolled my thumb over the screen. Reject. She tried my other thumb. Reject. She patiently took the prints of four other fingers from both hands. Reject. Out of all the prints she took, she only got one good print.

My fingerprints were fading! I could rob a bank and not get caught! If I were mangled in a car wreck, no one could identify me! I failed the test!

After fretting about this for some time, God thumped me on the head and said, "Your true identity is in Me." In Him I have a divine dog tag.

If I succeed, I belong to Him.
If I fail, I belong to Him.

No matter how old or sick Jeff got, or how faded his tags became, he was still ours. We knew him and loved him.

No matter how much we change over the years or how many times we get lost, we belong to God and He loves us.

Matt. 12:35

A good man reveals the rich treasures within him

Several weeks have gone by since we lost our two beautiful Golden Retrievers, Jeff and Jesse. The pain has not subsided and I wonder how long it will take for my heart to heal.

Jeff, the eight year old, was the larger of the two dogs. He was snow white, majestic and as gentle as a lamb. Jesse was my fifteen-year-old auburn girl. She was loyal, sweet and kind. Both were therapy dogs and had earned their Outstanding Therapy Dog Awards for making 338 visits in less than eighteen months. They spent time with nursing home residents, at-risk teens and children in all twelve grades. They visited inner city schools, spent many hours with special children and special adults, and had been assigned numerous Hospice patients. Jeff and Jesse loved me and my husband and they also loved as many other humans as they could fit in their day.

Last summer I noticed Jeff's abdomen expanding and thought he might be eating too much dog food. I cut his portions down, yet his girth widened. We made an appointment with the vet. He had a massive tumor. The doctor opened him up and removed an eleven-pound mass from my 100-pound boy. His incision would not heal, so they opened him up three more times. More cancer.

Jeff died on Tuesday, October 31, at 9:15 a.m.

Jesse mourned the loss of her close companion. She lost her hearing completely. She went blind. Her bodily functions ceased.

Jesse died on Tuesday, November 20, at 9:15 a.m.

Through my tears and disbelief and stabbing pain, I wondered: Jeffie-boy and Jesse-girl, what were you here to teach me that only your death could show me?

The answer was that my dogs did more living in their eight and fifteen years than most people do in a lifetime. They played. They dashed. They frolicked. They hugged and cuddled and kissed. They were full of joy. They loved every moment as though it was their last.

Jeff and Jesse's lives were a gift to me. Their deaths were also a gift to me. They showed me how important it is to slow down, to dance, to look up at the stars, to spend time with my family, to talk about God, to share my love and to trust.

For me to escape the gravity of despair on my own was an impossible task. God in his great mercy lifted me up on wings like eagles. He provided Living Water for me to drink. There was always power in His love.

Thank you, Jeff and Jesse, for showing me what God's unconditional love is like. I know for sure angels come in all forms.

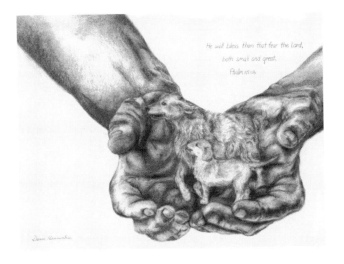

Some weeks ago I took Pete, our Lhasa Apso, to the veterinarian. Our young female vet was very sensitive and gentle, but Pete still wasn't sure about this, especially since he had been rescued just months ago. As the vet started to take Pete away, he turned and with his fuzzy paws reached for his mommy—me!

Since Pete was a rescue, I had guessed there was trauma in his past, but he knew I was his master and I loved him and he trusted me. Whatever he feared, if I was near, he felt safe.

I am Pete's refuge; God is my refuge.

Mother's Day always reminds me of my mom and recently has been a day of remembering and longing for her embrace, loving words and physical presence.

You see, a little over two years ago, my mom fell on Christmas day at church. She hit her head, which resulted in two real nice shiners. Fourteen days after her fall, she had a heart attack and was life-flighted to Columbus. After the heart catheterization and surgeries, we brought her home to heal.

In this six-week period, she was restless, hardly sleeping and at times seemed confused. Mom had always been in charge and insisted on remaining so. I did not know what to do. I was not ready for her to die. Our relationship was the best that it had ever been. I felt as though I was on a ship in rough water and could not get my sea legs.

Mom died on February 16th.

I reached for my Master.

I reached for His people, my Christian friends. God took care of what I couldn't. This unseen God gave me His strength. My friends offered prayer and counsel.

I learned a new lesson in faith. By faith I could reach for my Master. Unlike Pete, who could touch me and see me, I cannot touch or see my Master, but I know that He is my refuge, just like I am Pete's refuge.

I do not have to fear when I have a God like that.

"Even though I walk through the valley of the shadow of death I will fear no evil, for you are with me..."   *Psalm 23:4*

*Be still and know that I am God.
Psalm 46:10*

The words, "Be still," are usually not in my vocabulary, but God and Hospice has changed all of that. Jesse and Jeff were always Hospice dogs from the time they were young and passed their therapy dog test. Now Pete is an official therapy dog.

When we got Pete, he seemed especially glad to be part of our family. He had been stolen from a very abusive place and would probably have died had this wonderful rescuer not saved his life. (We never found out who rescued Pete). I am sure Pete did not know how great his danger was, but I know he was glad to be out of that bad place and into our home and yard.

We had Pete just a few months when he started choking uncontrollably. He stopped running and playing and then laid on our bed and did not want to be moved. We hurried him off to the vet who gave him medicine and sound advice on being still, resting and taking his pills.

We snuggled with him, prayed over him and cried that he might die in the night.

We kept on praying and petting him, holding him and talking to him. Soon he was back to his old, healthy self. He was not meant to die yet. God had more for him to do, and not just as Ken and Dianne's watchdog, but as a teacher and friend to very sick people.

Pete had a special Hospice patient named Carrie. Carrie was ninety-six years old, feeble, but with a very sharp mind. Sometimes I feel that God gave me more time with Pete to show me how important it was to take time with Carrie—to be still, to listen and to pray with her.

Carrie did not complain about her aging body or that she was in a nursing home. Sometimes she wondered why God had kept her alive so long. She had been close to death many, many times. When she was lonely in her quiet room, God reminded her that He was giving her a chance for stillness and reminded her to pray for the list of people He gave her each day.

Remembering Carrie petting Pete, reminds me that I need to thank God for our stillness. Through Carrie I have found purpose and peace.

During our weekly visit, Carrie told

me that God explained why He had not taken her to heaven yet. You see, Carrie was a pastor's wife for over forty years. She was still on earth to share her wisdom with me as I journeyed through life as a new pastor's wife.

Pete and I valued our weekly visits. We were still. We listened. We prayed. God was with us in that quiet nursing home room.

My goal is to live for God every day and to thank Him for the people in my life and for times of stillness.

We had a special 96 year old friend, Carrie, who lived at the nursing home. On Friday, December 12, 2008, she left this life and went to heaven to dance with Jesus.

Two days before Carrie's death, Pete and I went for our weekly visit expecting to share snacks together and acquire more advice on how to be a better pastor's wife. We found Carrie hanging on to life by a thread. Pete kept pulling on his leash, trying to get closer to her bed. He pulled so hard he was choking, so I let him off the lead. Up he went onto the bed and snuggled up close to Carrie. He just lay there quietly, looking at her with those big, brown, compassionate eyes. As I watched Pete with Carrie, I was touched by his loyalty to her and her loyalty to me.

Carrie's loyalty to her husband and children reminded me of the Old Testament story of Ruth. Ruth and Orpah, Naomi's daughters-in-law, lost both of their husbands. Naomi urged both women to find new husbands and start over and to not be burdened by an old woman like her. Orpah took the advice, but Ruth clung to Naomi and said, "Where you go I will go and where you stay I will stay. Your God will be my God. May the Lord deal with me be it ever so severely if anything but death separates you and me (Ruth 1:16-17)."

Pete goes where I go and stays where I stay. Carrie went where her husband went and stayed where he stayed.

Carrie told me to pledge faithfulness and loyalty to my husband, Ken. In any marriage, including mine, there are many temptations and opportunities to run off to greener pastures. She told me we have to rely on a combination of two things to keep us loyal: love for each other and love for God. Carrie said that in a God-centered marriage (and she stressed the words "God-centered"), God never fences us in; he always leaves a door open. We can choose to leave or we can be like Pete or Carrie and choose to stay. She reminded me that there is one thing we can be assured of—God is always faithful to us.

Carrie is in a much better place—no pain, no sorrow. Pete and I will miss our weekly visits with our sweet little friend, but we were blessed to spend time with her; we enjoyed each other immensely.

Have you ever considered the difference between how you see yourself and how God sees you?

I have and I have found it quite revealing. Viewing myself through Pete's eyes has reminded me of God's perspective—which does not always match up with my own.

Some days I wake up on the wrong side of the bed. I get up and look in the mirror. Unbelievable! Who is that woman staring back at me? Some gray hair, a few age spots and crow's feet. My eyes move down to my body. Bicycle tire around my waist, lack of muscle tone in the arms, probably even bad breath and body odor. We all have days like this, don't we?

Pete does not seem to see what I see in the mirror. Every morning he snuggles up to kiss me, bounds out to the kitchen ready for his walk, tail wagging furiously. Never once does he appear to look down on me for my less-than-movie star appearance. Pete never cares what I look like on the outside. All he sees is his master. He is concerned about my heart. He is focused on my essence—the "me" God created to last forever.

Last month, seven special men visited our church from a group home in Wooster, Ohio. Pete greeted each man individually as lovable and worthy creatures made by God:

<u>Neal</u> did not want to let Pete go.

<u>Tim</u> gave Pete attention without words.

<u>Steven</u> said, "I love you."

<u>Bo</u> smiled down on Pete.

<u>Bill</u> pulled Pete in close.

<u>Gary</u> waited until Pete reached out to him.

<u>Mickey</u> rested is forehead against Pete's and savored the closeness.

Think of these seven responses. Don't they remind you of how God perceives us?

<u>He</u> does not let go.

<u>He</u> connects.

<u>He</u> smiles.

<u>He</u> is attentive to our needs.

<u>He</u> says, "I love you."

<u>He</u> waits for us.

<u>He</u> pulls us in close.

Pete said to these gentlemen, "Your outer man isn't nearly as important as your inner man."

Pete has taught me that what makes

me loveable and worthy is not my external body that decays. What makes me loveable and worthy is my heart. My heart defines who I am. God sees that and so does Pete.

Watching these seven gentlemen with Pete and listening to their conversations was pure wonder and joy!

Whenever welcomes
a little child like this in
My name is welcoming Me.

Mark 9:37

I was watching Pete eat his breakfast the other day. If he is really hungry, he will finish off the bowl of food instantly. Sometimes, when his tummy is happy and not empty, he will check out what is in the bowl and push the bowl with his nose until it is hidden in a corner. Pete knows just what he needs to be a healthy growing dog. He does not grumble or plead for more. He is satisfied with enough.

God knows just what we need to keep us spiritually healthy and growing in Him. Do you ever grumble and plead for more, instead of being satisfied with enough?

The children of Israel had to learn to be satisfied with enough when God gave them their daily manna in the desert. Moses warned them not to hoard their manna for the next day. Those who hoarded found their day-old manna smelly and filled with worms. God wanted his people to trust Him for their daily bread on a daily basis—just like Pete trusts me.

Remember the Lord's Prayer? "Give us each day our daily bread (Luke 11:3)." As an adult, do you ask, "Please, God, just give me enough for today?" or do you say, "I want more money and power and fame."

Like Pete, I am blessed to have a Master who provides for my needs. If my eyes stray from God, my focus is on wants. I do not just want what is in my dish; I want the whole twenty pound bag of dog food! Perhaps God knows that we do not need more—we just need more of Him.

My husband and I used to call Pete "The Great Houdini." Do you remember the famous escape artist, Houdini? Well, Pete was the dog version of this exciting artist. Pete would climb and jump and wedge his little body through a slightly opened door. Just when we thought we had tackled every escape situation, he found a new way out.

I used to love to read in the back yard and have Pete on the bench next to me, off the leash. While I was engrossed in a book, though, Pete would slither off the bench and be halfway up our street before I sensed his absence. Determined to thwart him, I barricaded off the north side of the house with fence and trellis. The little stinker turned his attention to the south side of the house and off he went, either chasing an Amish buggy or checking out the customers at the neighborhood grocery store.

Pete had not ignored his boundaries to be bad or because he wanted to leave his nice cozy home. He was curious and wanted a squirrel or a bird or a horse— "good things." Boundaries stood in the way of his pleasure. Since he was a dog, he did not know boundaries were for his benefit, so he would not be hurt or even killed.

As a teenager and young adult, I did not realize boundaries were for my benefit either.

Beginning in the eighth grade, I struggled with some extra weight. In my sophomore year, I dated a guy who wished me to be svelte and popular. I took things too far and by the summer between my junior and senior year, my 5' 5 1/2" body frame of 125 pounds dropped to 100 pounds. I developed an eating disorder called anorexia. If anorexia goes unchecked, it can lead to serious health problems or even death, like it did for the famous singer Karen Carpenter.

I wanted to be thin. I wanted to be in control. I wanted to chase birds and squirrels and horses like Pete did. Had I stayed in the healthy boundaries of taking care of my body as if it were a temple, I would not have been so obsessive about my weight.

A very wise and caring person came into my life, took me aside and very gently told me that if I continued on this downhill spiral I would die. He helped me to seek

God's divine intervention, to pray unceasingly and to love myself as God loved me. At first I was resentful. What right did he have to interfere in my life? Then I realized that he wanted to save me from untold harm. He knew better than I and his fence was a sign of love.

God knows better, too. He sets fences around us to keep us from harm and sometimes from death. God's fence is made up of His Spirit and His Word. While we are out chasing "good things" like Pete did, God sees the danger and gives us boundaries.

Pete does not try to escape anymore and I have less of a desire to be thin and thinner. It is much nicer to be safe in God's fences, to be secure and calm and bask in His love, just like Pete basks in my love and in my boundaries.

Last August, Ken and I went to a dinner theater with friends. Because we had extra time we made a side trip to an antique store in Berlin, Ohio. In close proximity was a pet store so we went in to buy a toy and some dog food for Pete. Puppies, puppies and more puppies were in the store. A little white bundle of fur came over to greet us. As soon as we inhaled that beautiful odor of an eight-week old puppy, we were smitten.

We named her Mary Magdalene Hammontree.

Puppies make you roll in the grass and giggle. They can chew and whine all night and pee on the floor and poop in the corner.

Puppies cause you to look up at a million stars, to stop and watch a squirrel tight-rope walk across the electric wires and make you take time to smell the roses and spring flowers. They teach you to enjoy all God's handiwork.

Mary has a special way of vocalizing. It sort of sounds like the moaning E.T. did in the movie before he said, "E.T. phone home."

Mary runs, jumps and bounces when she walks in the snow and looks like some bizarre living bowling ball rolling down our sidewalk.

Sometimes it is hard to snuggle with a nipping, wiggling pup, especially for my husband. When Mary sees his George Washington nose she just has to have a bite of it. Then she slobbers on him real good.

When we come home, Mary runs to each of us and jumps into our arms and greets us. She knows how much we love her and she is eager to get the attention and affection she has not had all day. But sometimes I am not as eager to see Mary as she is to see me. There are days when I am tired or busy or frazzled and overwhelmed.

When it comes to taking time with God, am I as excited to leap into His arms as Mary is to leap into mine? Am I willing to stop and listen when He speaks or do I let tiredness or busyness intrude on my relationship with Him?

I confess that it is easy for my focus to shift to my own needs and not take the time to love my God as I should.

Love is first on Mary's priority list.

She never lets the stuff of life intrude. I pray that I will take the time to love, to be attentive to my family and to leap into God's arms every day.

It takes commitment and sacrifice to have Mary. We play, we rest and we have long conversations. If I can receive this much joy with Mary, think of how much exceedingly great joy I can have from God if I commit and sacrifice for Him and play and rest and have long conversations with Him.

Because your love is better than life, my lips will glorify you.
Psalm 63:3

Ecclesiastes 3:8

Pete was an only child (dog) for a while and rarely got into serious mischief—until Mary, a Shih Tzu and Esther, a Lhasa Apso, came along. Their motto was "anything is possible." Pete, Mary and Esther were not bad dogs, but the combination of the three together with idle time brought out the "animal" in them.

In our private section of the Bed & Breakfast there is a bathroom, a bedroom, and a computer room. Let the three dogs have "private time" and the two wastebaskets would be emptied, the windows would be slobbered on, all their favorite things would be hidden under the bed and several plants would be involuntarily pruned. I asked the dogs why they would hide a sock, underwear, a bone, Kleenex, a clothespin and several dollars under the bed. I half expected them to verbalize excuses, but their only response was a silly looking grin—like Austrians who pretend not to speak English while you are hopelessly trying to communicate in their German tongue.

Pete would never have done any of these doggie deeds on his own. What if something had harmful consequences like chewing on an electric cord or eating a poisonous leaf?

As with puppies, the people we choose as our friends can influence our actions. Some are good and some are bad.

Proverbs 13:20 says, "He who walks with the wise grow wise, but a friend of fools suffers harm."

When I was young, a neighborhood boy made me feel bad if I did not torment the elderly lady next door or if I did not take candy out of the cupboards when my mom was not looking. Peer pressure, whether you are young or mature, is usually nurtured by "a friend of fools." Giving into peer pressure is not good. Being manipulated by someone is not good. When an action feels bad, do what Hebrews 10:24-25 says, "Spur one another on toward love and good deeds and encourage one another."

It absolutely matters who you choose to spend time with. Our friends can influence us for better or for worse.

When my girls were little, they were encouraged to visit older folks. Soon some of their friends made visits with them. They would laugh, hear stories, exchange gifts and share homemade snacks. Positive peer pressure spurred the girls and their friends toward love and good deeds.

One older dog and two little puppies came together to wreak havoc.

A bunch of little girls came together to brighten the lives of the older generation and discovered the blessings that followed.

Choose your friends wisely.

Think of the possibilities when you choose God as your friend to spend time with.

Mary loves to play fetch. She has many toys to play with, but her favorite one is BEAR. BEAR is always dirty. He is missing a leg and part of his tail. BEAR used to be cute, but since Mary claimed him, he is ragged, chewed, loved and ugly.

Mary knows the names of all her toys and usually brings them on command. One Tuesday I said, "Mary, bring BEAR." She raced to her toy box and brought octopus.

"No, Mary," I scolded, "bring BEAR." She ran off again and brought mouse. "Bring BEAR," I repeated.

Off and on all day I gave the fetch command, but Mary fetched every toy but BEAR. She knew my command but refused to obey. I refused to play anymore until she obeyed.

On Wednesday I said, "Bring BEAR." She looked up at me with her warm brown eyes then ran through the house and brought me BEAR. She climbed onto my lap and lavished me with lots of happy noises and wet kisses. "Please forgive me," she seemed to say.

Normally Mary is faithful and obedient. When she is disobedient, our connection is strained, and we do not enjoy each other as much. But when Mary seeks forgiveness, and I forgive her, our relationship is restored with joy.

Sometimes I am like Mary with Jesus. Sometimes He asks me to lay certain things at His feet and I balk at the command. I say to Jesus, "I can take care of this," or "I do not want to obey."

Sometimes Jesus says, "Bring me your fears," and I fetch my children and lay them at His feet.

"Bring me your fears," He says, and I lay my husband at His feet.

"Dianne, bring me your fears," He commands. When He addresses me by name, I respond immediately.

I love Jesus and He loves me. I love feeling close to Him, talking to Him and experiencing His guidance. God does not forget about me when I am disobedient any more than I forget about Mary. But disobedience hurts. Disobedience breaks our closeness. I will try to obey when He says in His still small voice, "Dianne, bring me your fears."

How my dogs, Pete, Esther & Mary, will celebrate Mother's Day:

1. Rise at 5:30 a.m. and give me a wet-nose greeting
2. Go out to pee on the world
3. Make poopy
4. Sniff poopy
5. Seriously think about eating poopy
6. Eat funny looking bugs instead
7. Throw up bugs
8. Drink out of magic well (La Toilette)
9. Take a 3-mile walk and greet every tombstone in the cemetery
10. Take a 17 hour nap
11. Start over with #1

Esther is blind. We suspected her eyesight might not be normal, but never in our wildest dreams did we think she was blind. We look at her actions differently now. If she softly growls at someone or something, it is because she is frightened, not vicious. When we walk her we have to keep her on a short leash, so she does not run into a tree or a sign. When we feed her, we sit her bowl right in front of her nose.

Walking Esther is a wonderful adventure. She hears me open the closet to get my jacket. She hears me get the leash off the kitchen hook and fetch the doggie bags out of the drawer. I may still be in my pajamas, but Esther does not see this. All she knows is that these sounds mean it is time for a walk.

Early on in our stroll she comes upon a discarded Bud Lite can – yuck! Next she finds M & M's left over from kids playing outside – yum! Shortly, we come to a dead stop. Esther has her rear in the air, her head face down on the pavement and she is striking gently at a bug – fun! Soon after the bug incident, she begins tiptoeing quietly, nose in the air. Road kill – smelly!

As our adventure continues, we come to the town creek. She listens to the water gurgling, she smells the wet moss and the wild flowers and she feels the cool water as she lays her whole body down on the smooth rocks. God's beautiful grasses and flowers frame her little body as tadpoles and frogs swim by. Esther is so content. It does not matter that she cannot see. All of her joys cost nothing. All of her joys were created by God at this moment, at this place.

Before we turn towards home, we enter the cemetery. Esther seems to be on a mission, like she knows which graves need a visit: a baby, a mommy, a World War II veteran. They all get a sniff and a kiss. As Esther reverently lies at my feet, I stand in awe of my God and His beauty and I pray that God will help me be more perceptive to people's needs.

We are almost home now and as we approach the partially opened back door, I release her leash and say, "Go get Daddy." Esther perfectly maneuvers through the door, kitchen, family room, and dining room and barrels into the library to see Ken. She seems to say to him, "Seize the day. Every minute of every day needs to be celebrated."

Esther may be blind, but she can see God's works. "Stop and smell the roses," she teaches. "You don't need eyes to appreciate an adventure."

Spontaneity. Puppies are great little spontaneous beings. For instance, last June, early on a Sunday morning at our old farmhouse, my husband Ken and I were getting ready to go to church. The puppies, Mary and Esther, and boy-dog Pete, were wide awake, fed and walked. Ken got ready first so he hopped over to his office to finish some last minute preparations. Ten minutes later he rushed in the side door, left the door ajar and ran up the stairs to retrieve a few more supplies.

Where is Esther? We both ran to the open door and watched as blind Esther tore down the county road in pursuit of an Amish horse and buggy. Since I was shoeless, I ran back into the kitchen to get my beautiful green-stained lawn mowing shoes. I noticed that Mary was okay and safe. She was having a wonderful time playing with a funny looking toy. Oops! This was not a toy. She was tearing into George Washington's beautiful white, curled, powdered wig! I grabbed the wig from Mary, put her in her kennel and ran after Esther in my stunning white sundress and green lawn-mowing shoes. By now, Esther was at the bottom of the road and the only reason I caught her was because she stopped to eat horse-puckey.

Finally, Ken and I got all three dogs kenneled and calmly walked over to the church. We were greeted by hysterical "Good mornings" and "Do you always dress up to go jogging?"

Spontaneity. Will you be spontaneous? Can you be like the puppies and go after your heart's desire?

If a friend asks you out to dinner and you have a million things to do at home— go. Things will wait. If you are shopping and see a mom struggling to pay on a lay-away—anonymously pay on her bill. If you are free at breakfast, add a little cinnamon to your french toast and invite a lonely neighbor over to chat. If your spouse asks you to visit his family—get in the car.

Be spontaneous with God. Thank Him for everything He has given you. Thank Him for a time to help, a time to visit and a time to enjoy friends and family. Thank God for the miracle of Christmas and for the chance to start all over again.

Remember who you are and trust that

God will get you through the storms.
> Be a puppy.
> Be joyful.
> Be spontaneous—today!

Unto Thee I lift up my eyes...
Psalms 123:1

January is a time of reflection for me…remembering the past sixty years and the people and the dogs that have been part of my life. I recall the dogs from my childhood to the present in this way:

Jet=Kindness

Jet, my childhood mutt, was kindness. I learned so much by watching the way she rejoiced in life's simplest moments. Every morning was Christmas morning. Every run was the best run. Every dinner was the best dinner. She taught me to take time to celebrate the gifts God gave me in childhood and to be kind to others.

Rusty=Patience

Both Rusty and I learned patience during our ten years together. We came together when I was a newly-married full-time worker. Rusty did not get the attention and affection he needed all day, so potty training was quite a chore. I must confess that there were times when I would come home from work and barely say "hi" to him. I might pat him on the head, then get in the car and head to the grocery store or laundromat. I was busy, overwhelmed and lonely. My patience waned. Rusty peed.

We both got better and became more patient with each other. Patience takes time!

Jesse=Self-Control

Jesse taught me to wait to control my thoughts and emotions. She was always with me—in the car, in the house and in the bathroom. During my anxious moments, she would snuggle up to me, head to head, and say, "This is only a moment; it is not the rest of your life." I would immediately calm down, breathe and tackle the problem, head to head.

Jill= Goodness

Even though Jill only lived for four years, she taught me to enjoy life, even the stressful things, because we only have this moment.

Jeff=Love

The more I observed Jeff, the more confident I became that God sent him to me to show me what unconditional love is all about.   Jeff   was   innocence,   loyalty, affection, grace and love.   He was an exceptional creature and I miss him.

Joy=Joy

Joy was joyful even though she had nothing—no home, no food and no loving family. She was like the birds in Matthew 6:26. They did not worry about food or shelter. They trusted God to take care of them. She reminded me that we are all very important to God and that we need to be joyful, no matter what our circumstances.

Pete=Gentleness

Pete and I go for a walk in the woods to quiet the noise of the world. When we are together in the quiet, I can take time to ask God, "What would you have me do today?" Pete just sits beside me as a gentle spirit and waits until I receive an answer.

Mary=Peace

Mary loves me just as I am. Often I do not realize who I am meant to be because I have been very busy trying to live out someone else's ideas. Mary teaches me that other people and their opinions hold no power over my destiny. She teaches me to love myself and be peaceful about that choice.

Esther=Faithfulness

I have learned a lot from Esther in just one year. She has shown me what a faithful friend is. It does not matter if I am upset, tired or happy. Esther is always at the kitchen door to meet me, greet me and protect me, even though she is blind.

Nine dogs and their nine virtues equal the nine fruits of the spirit in Galatians 5:22. Please look for kindness, love, joy, peace, patience, goodness, faithfulness, gentleness and self-control in your family and friends.

Looking for virtues in others is very rewarding.